Falling Endlessly

Angel Andrades Montanez

to the part of me
who believed in a love so
reckless it almost killed me.

Grand Exit

You quickly started to change
every aspect of my life,
I could no longer recognize the person
I was before I met you.
You molded me into your own creation,
I lost bits and pieces of myself being with you.
You stripped me of the only sanity I had left,
And when you made your grand exit out of my
life...
 You took who I was with you, I'm afraid I'll
never find myself again.

Land Of The Lost

Now every time you say you love me
it feels like it's going to be the last time,
I hear those words, and once again
I find myself lost in your piercing eyes
I never thought our last kiss
would actually be our last
I would've held you tighter...
As time passes I'm afraid
you will find someone more passionate than I
But the love I have for you ,
that you will always remember
The bitter sweet taste I left behind ..
In between our arguments I wanted to say "shut
up I love you"
I wanted to stop being foolish and arrogant
I was fighting my pride
I wanted to express every emotion,
and every feeling I stored inside
You'll never know how I truly feel
Because words are just words,
and thoughts are just thoughts
And my actions did not speak loud enough.

Heartache

My chest tightened
my throat was on fire,
I was holding back all the things
I wanted to say,
 I knew nothing would be good enough
 to make you stay.
I will never understand why you left,
I will never forget how you hurt me
I will always remember why I love you ...

Fight For You

Everyone would ask me why I hadn't
given up on you
I had a simple answer
It was something about the desire to do better
that I saw in your eyes
It made me fight for you .
I desired happiness
more than anything in the world
You filled the void
no one else could fill
The more I denied it
the more pain demanded to be felt.

Asylum

Since the day she died,
He could never leave the hotel.
Everywhere he went, her face followed,
But then it got to the point where
He could see her entire body and even
Feel her presence around him.
The rear view mirror was haunted with her
smiling face.
He could feel it throughout his senses, even the
taste.
He couldn't take it!
Didn't feel like he'd make it,
But one day he did something different, he
embraced it.
She was the one who gave him his drive, but
she'd driven him crazy.
He didn't even feel alive, but he felt sane seeing
her on the daily.
Shots and pills just to get him through the day,
but that only
Made him hear everything that she had to say.
The doctors noticed that he would dance with
someone by noon.
He wouldn't stop; even if someone came into the
room.

I drove you crazy , I know I did ..
I wanted you to feel the pain I felt when I was
alive .
I wanted to haunt your every thought,
and fill every empty void so you would feel
distraught.
I needed to make you my prisoner & flood your
mind with memories
that you would never be able to relive again .
All I remember is the words you muttered
before you stabbed me in the back and watched
me bleed..
after that day you could never leave the hotel...
You were left insane, dancing alone at noon to
the music we used to play.

Silence

Loving you wasn't difficult until,
I had to love you in silence.

No one said a word,
Our silence spoke for the both of us...
That's how our story ended.

Falling For You

I fell in love with the way you looked at the world, as if it wasn't ending .

Coffee

It was 6am I hadn't slept in days,
I was stuck in bed in that same position for
almost 4 hours.

I laid still, eyes shut tight, one hand over my head
as if that was going to prevent me from having
you on my mind.

I finally decided to get up...
I stood there, tired of our memories dancing
around in my brain.

I wish one cup of coffee.
could get rid of this existential pain,

But instead, it leaves this bitter taste in my
mouth, just like you did when you left.

It's like no matter how much sugar I put into my
coffee, I will be left with that masking taste and
no matter what I do to forget you ...
you will never be forgotten.

Trust

I thought you were going to be different,
I should've trusted your actions not your words.

Like Magic

"When our eyes meet,
I feel like we've exchanged 1,000 words,
That's why I say "I could look at you all day,
without saying a word."

Eye Contact

The sun illuminates the eyes,
so you know they were gifted by the skies.

Blind Love

I was a slave to you, blinded by love.

Swimming

We swam through treacherous waters,
Risking it all...
For a love we thought would last forever.

Lost And Found

The love she lost was found in you ...

Later

What if later
becomes never?

Missed Calls

I long for the day
I won't wait
for your call anymore.

Why Do I Still Care?

I hate how much I still care.

Forged In Flames

The flames consumed her,
Barely hanging on
The fumes were intoxicating,
Turning her into ashes.

Wisdom

You were strong enough to leave,
and wise enough to never look back.

Beautiful

Wouldn't it be beautiful if we could start over,
make peace with our past and rewrite our story.

Pain

Your thorns were lodged into my heart,
You were hurting me,
but at the same time keeping me alive.

Grow

It all happened so you could grow,
The mistakes you thought would make you want
to end your life...
Are the reason you're strong enough to keep
living.

You

I was your strength,
you were my weakness.
3/12/19

Damaged Hearts

"I'm damaged, you don't want that."
My darling, we all are.

Solitude

I used to be so afraid
of living my life without you...
Look at me now,
fearless.

In A Matter of Seconds

It took you 2 seconds to walk away from me,
It took me almost 2 years to heal from that.

Home

There's something so familiar about you...
From strangers to friends,
From friends to strangers.
You still feel like home to me.

Rest In Paradise

I was left in a state of shock when I got the news,
You are in heaven now.
I still haven't processed that you're gone,
I'm not good at dealing with loss.
I have a feeling you're at peace now.
No more suffering, for you.

Break Up

Do you know how long I went without listening to music, just because every song I used to play made me think of you?
Do you know how many places I avoided? just so I wouldn't accidently bump into you.
Yet, I'm still not over you. One tends to feel like they've been broken, and that is as honest as that phrase gets, because getting "up" always feels impossible.
All you really feel is as if you are endlessly falling with no end to this pain in sight.

Peaceful Solitude

I've found so much peace alone now,
company feels so unfamiliar unlike it used to.

Broken

There was nothing left...
She only had a stream of tears.
Broken fragments of her heart everywhere.
Her face was rested on a cold hard floor;
Yet it sent a message of how she could be.
Cold hearted, and silent...

Selfless

I hope you find happiness,
even if it's not with me.

You Are Seen

I saw you for who you were,
not for who everyone else wanted you to be,
and my eyes held no judgment.

The Day You Left

I'll never forget the day you left,
you had a blue sweatshirt on and your luggage in
hand,
that was the last time you gave me a long-lasting
hug,
you cried on my shoulder and told me to "never
give up".
I let a few tears rush down my face as I got ready
for everything to change,
 & after that day nothing was ever the same…
I tried so hard to be okay,
 but I could never adjust to that empty space.
 You were gone and with you I felt safe…

Time

It takes time,
Sometimes years to understand,
how the pain that felt
like it was beating you to death
gave you the strength to live.

If You Came Back

The problem is I would let you back in so easily,
No matter how ruthless you were
when you walked out on me.

I'm Listening

To hear you talk about someone else,
the way you used to talk about me,
made me question everything.

Karma

Next time you think about hurting someone,
Remember karma has a funny way of showing
you exactly what you made them go through.

Don't Look For Me

You will never find me where you left me...

Fly

The wings I needed to fly,
you cut off ...
Because you were too insecure
to let me go anywhere without you.

Absence Of Oneself

I feel like I lost her ...
The girl I was before you put your hands on
me,
The one who saw you as the answer to her
prayers.
How is it possible that the person that makes
me feel so unsafe,
Could make me feel safe while they're
holding me...
How insane to pray for utter destruction.

A Collective Perception

I see the world in black, and white.
Somehow the only color left, we find in each
other's eyes.

How Do We Shelter From Ourselves?

I think of you in the calm before the storm, I remember how frightened you would get when the lightning struck. You held on to me, as if here in this space, safety would remain forever, but time proved us wrong.

Love Forged In Fire

Our love grew like a flame,
We sat and dwelled in our desires,
unafraid of the blazing fire we could create.
Or the risks that come with following a feeling,
 and ignoring our mistakes.
Like a wildfire It spread,
consuming us whole for a risk we were willing to take,
even when the consequences meant we were no longer safe.

Worth The Fall

After getting my heart torn out of my chest one
too many times,
I questioned all the emotions that came with
being in love.
Was it ever love?
I'm terrified of falling again...
It's like I can't stop myself, no matter how much I
try to resist...
your words become more profound
As you speak them, my mind convinces me
of all the reasons why you are worth falling for.
I find myself lost...
in the sound of your voice.

Natural Beauty

You were filled with so many insecurities
that blinded you from seeing
the beauty in your reflection.

Depression

It was destroying me from the inside out...
I felt deserted.
Those mornings in which waking up felt like a
nightmare,
A constant torment,
Falling asleep was my escape from reality...
 or at least a little while.

Healing

Healing begins when you start to strip away all
the parts of you that no longer serve you.
Cutting ties with your past,
Remembering you are no longer there
anymore...

Anxiety

Who would I be?
if not for my anxiety,
Who would I be?
if I was able to speak in front of a large crowd
freely,
with no impediment in my speech.
How would it feel?
to wake up with my heart beating at a normal
rate.
How would it feel?
To walk past a group of people and feel no
shame...
To live without anxiety is a dream, I'm
determined to see it as a reality.

To See You Again

It's not that I don't want to see you,
I just don't know if I'm ready.
 Are we ever though? The more we attempt to
avoid,
do the feelings to confront what you've been
running from ever go away?
In the absence of what no longer serves us, we
learn why.
We learn to accept what we need and neglected
before so that when confronted by our past or
our fears we reap from our lessons we've
learned because this kind of growth when
staring what at some point had you at your knees
in the eyes and smiling says more than my words
ever could and louder than what you may think
is silent.

Confronting My Past

I sat near the water...
Pen and paper in hand,
Writing down all the reasons why my life wasn't
going as planned.
I was young then, I wasn't aware that I, myself
could take control of my life.
I was nowhere near healing from the torment I
had endured for several years in silence, that's
the thing about staying quiet.
If you don't speak you will forever be bound to
that constant torture, and resentment that comes
from bottling things up inside. I put the pen
down, I reached for the lighter in my pocket,
debating if I should turn that paper into ash...
my finger slid back exposing the flame, I put it a
little closer to where my writing caught on fire,
slowly burning away the reasons why.

Young

I wanted to speak up, believe me I did, but I felt like if I opened my mouth to speak the truth, no one would believe my word against his.

Clarity

That conversation you've been avoiding,
Is the one you need to have.
You say you want closure,
Maybe you aren't ready to say goodbye,
To close that chapter of your life,
So you avoid that talk...

You know it's the only thing keeping you
from continuing this journey.
You just don't want to do it alone.
You're so much stronger than you think ...
Fighting each and every battle in silence
Instead of resorting to violence.
You're strong,
I admire the way you fight,
You are resilient,
You are light.

Catching Fire

"Please light the fire."
My soul exclaimed!
She reached for the lighter, and exposed the flame.
I was trapped in delusion,
My soul in chains..
"Please light the fire"
I cried out.
I let myself slip away
Burning into ashes
As my fears escaped...

Rain

I looked up at the sky,
Dark clouds were forming...
I could smell that a heavy rain was
approaching,
Maybe to wash away all of my sins.
As the water trickled down my face.
I could feel the pain wash away and leave my
body.
The fragments of my heart that were broken,
Became whole again...
I was being cleansed of my past self; only to
be born again.

I Love You

The world is so much more beautiful with you in mine,
I can't deny that I've already said "I love you" in my head more than a million times.

Losing You

I wanted you, but the odds were never in our favor.

Skin

With just one look,
It felt like I was trapped in your skin.

Scorpion

Put together like a perfect melody, the inner
strength of a warrior... Fighting battles like a
soldier... eyes piercing into the souls of
everyone encountered the wit of a master.
Her voice resounded in my head, but her
venom stings; like it was meant for me.

Look At Me Now

If you could see me now…
I'm not the same as I was before.
If you could see me now…
You'd see the light in my eyes,
You'd see the way I've grown.
If you could see me now…
There would be no doubt in your mind that I
will accomplish my dreams,
It will be set in stone.

If only you could see me now…

New Friends

They say never to talk to strangers,
So we go through life with many missed
connections.
Overthinking the risk of a friendly hello,
And missing the reward of an unfamiliar
comfort;
I wish it was easier to make meaningful
connections.
In my most recent days I find it hard to trust
pure intentions, how unbearable.

Swim

She had a cold embrace as she pulled me in.
Every time she pushed me, I'd fall deep enough
to swim.
My body never felt so submerged before.
When I turned, I was moving further away from
the shore...

He had a warm embrace as I pulled him in.
My heart was cold, I wasn't strong enough to
swim.
My body never felt so weak before...
I laid isolated at the shore, as he swam further
away from me...

I'll See Light Again

Those nights that I would want to last
forever, I would dread for the sun to come up
& have to wake up to the task that I called
life. I would find refuge in the night, in a
silence that brought me comfort.
Maybe I was just unhappy in my own skin,
and when the day would come again, I'd be
exposed of my sins, my past and pain longing
for a peace I felt I could never regain.
Now I just remember those days for they are
behind me, and everything so far has
unraveled in perfect timing.
A reminder that what feels like will last
forever, doesn't, not even your darkest days,
they will see light too.

My Mind

I will never forget the day I opened up my mind
to you...
The day I let you in completely,
You explored all the corners of my mind,
Searching for something that was never really
there.

With you I exist

I've never felt more alive than I do when
you're in my space...
Your energy brings me peace, I call you my
safe place.

Walking through fire

Hot as hell,
Barefoot on the fire...
It burned to the touch.
I continued on my path,
I know if I crossed it I'd reach you;
So I went on my way,
Walking through the fires of hell,
To get to heaven, just to meet you.

Vertigo

As soon as I step foot outside,
I lose balance.
As the world collides,
My head is spinning,
This is my demise.
I lose balance,
Now I'm staring at the sky.

Storm

You were a storm,
Rage consumed you...
Your eyes turned a fiery red,
Your words were like venom.
We don't make sense.
Calm like the soft waves that would crash
into shore,
I brought serenity to you.
You brought destruction!

Me Vs Me

I was so close to giving up...
I felt like I was taking up space
In a world that had no room for me...
A lost cause, a disappointment,
Yet I was always reminded that
Life was worth living.
Why couldn't I believe it?

Trauma

I was done explaining myself,
Having to repeat the same story a countless
number of times.
Only to be traumatized all over again...
Each time in more detail
You still weren't pleased with my responses,
It felt like I was begging for you to believe
me.

Anger Issues

I could feel my body getting overheated,
my head was pounding like it was about to
explode...
I was no longer in control of my body,
I started to see red.
Losing control,
That was something I never wanted to
experience again...
My darkest side,
There is nothing I can do to pull myself out of
that black hole I fall into when my anger
spikes.

Sunsets

I love when the sky turns a fiery red,
A vibrant orange with a hint of yellow...
I take out my camera to snap a picture so it
will last longer.
I can always go back to it, and feel an ounce
of what I felt in that moment.
As all my worries disappeared,
And my head was clear.
My thoughts went silent...
For just one moment,
I was one with the sky.

What I Want

We wanted completely different things.
You wished for an apartment in the city,
And it was my dream to live in a house in the
suburbs...
Our future seemed to be all I craved,
and at the same it seemed to be the furthest
thing, from what I really wanted.

Love Yourself

Losing you taught me how to love myself.

Miles Apart

Even if we're 744 miles apart you're closer to my heart than anyone has ever been.

Breathe

Breathe
That was the one word that kept me going.
When I thought about breaking, I would
whisper "breathe" under my breath. To
remind myself that I could never give up.

Attached

My heart was more attached to you than I
thought.
Seeing you again opened wounds,
I was certain were healed.
I wanted to scream, cry... But all I could
manage to do was smile.

Home

I want to explore the world with you,
I want us to build a foundation that would
never be broken.
For as long as you're with me I know where
my home will forever be.

Little Lies

But I'd be lying if I said I didn't miss her...

Remember

It got to the point where I could no longer see
myself,
I lost touch with who I was.
Trying to put fragments of memories back
together,
Missing pieces to the puzzle I could not solve.
I spent my nights wishing I could remember
the girl I once was.

Last Forever

I've learned over time that beautiful things
don't always last forever,
We all have our end.
Our beating hearts will one day come to a
complete stop,
Most people are scared of death.
I think what I'm most scared of is leaving
without ever feeling alive.

Since You've Been Gone

Once again, I'm taken back to that day,
You're so different now.
I look at you and I don't see the person I first
met, I see pain in those eyes that used to light
up the world...
You went dark.

In memory of you

Memories exist so that we can relive moments that won't last forever.

Did you know that I love you?

There's a million reasons why...
But none of them could compare to the actual
feeling.
Did you know that I love you?
It was so unexpected,
The way our story unraveled.
The direct approach
The right answers
I didn't plan this,
But my heart chose.

Where is my love?

The feeling I longed for since I was a child...
I gave every ounce of my love away,
in hopes that it would be returned to me
someday.
I started to grow older developing a fear of
rejection,
the absence of love; a fear of connection.

Love Letter To Myself

You have to remember,
that the mirror is not always
going to show you what you want to see...
There will be days where you won't be
pleased with your appearance,
and there will be days where you'll see the
beauty everyone else sees.

Don't be so hard on yourself,
you are not difficult to love...
You deserve more than this world could ever
give you. You are deserving of all the good
things that happen to you.

May

I never liked my birthday.
I hated the idea of their being one specific day where all the attention was on me. I felt so much pressure even if it was my birthday. I felt like I needed to make sure everyone who attended my birthday was having the best times. Most of the time I couldn't even enjoy it because I was too busy paying attention to everyone else.
Eventually I just gave up. Eventually I treated the day I was born as if it was just another regular day.

Last Goodbye

I gazed into your eyes one last time,
With all the love in the world
I knew you were no longer for me...
It hurt to admit it,
But I couldn't keep lying to myself,
Thinking we would ever be what we used to
be...

Never Ending Nights

There were nights where I felt like the sun
would never rise for me again...
Like I would be stuck living in complete
darkness
Surrounded by my biggest fears,
Collecting all my tears.

Salt In the Wound

It never healed, the pain you inflicted on my heart, the tears were impossible to wash away. The scars that will never fade... That's what you left behind, as soon as you made your way out of my life.

Red Flags

I guess when you love somebody that much,
The red flags don't really matter...
You overlook so many things until your heart is
shattered.

Breaking Down My Walls

You bring out the parts of me I thought I would never get to meet, parts of me that I had never seen before.

To Be Put Back Together

Sometimes you need things to fall apart so they
can be put back together.

Last Forever

And even when we fight, I want to pull you in and
embrace you.
I know this feeling of anger won't last,
But I want you forever ..

Lust For Love

I lusted for your love, it was the only thing that could save me...

Change

You quickly started to change every aspect of my life
I could no longer recognize the person I was before I
met you
You molded me into your own creation
I lost bits and pieces of myself being with you
You stripped me of the only sanity I had left
And when you made your grand exit out of my life
You took who I was with you. I'm afraid I'll never see
her again.

Insecurities

I love all of the things you say you hate about
yourself ...
I'm in love with every single one of your
insecurities, vulnerability is perfection.

Perfect Image

The perfect image I had of you in my head was tainted by all the lies you fed me while I was starving for the truth.

Escape

I've tried to escape you for years.
You're the past that haunts me still.
Chasing me, trapping me,
Like nightmares I can't wake up from.
Your face follows me around…
Imitating the shadows;
Of what we used to call love.

Time

Forever doesn't seem to be long enough,
Every minute spent with you is precious.
Every moment without you...
I can feel the emptiness.
Your presence is impossible to be away from.
You're like a drug I can't escape from.
The Consequences of Your Actions
For you to give your body just like that to another,
How could you say I was still on your mind...
After everything you put me through
It didn't matter what you left behind.

Are You There?

My mind takes me back to that forbidden
place.
When those memories hit,
I pray they will be erased from my brain.
You were supposed to take care of me in my
youth,
Instead I took care of you.
I don't blame you for being absent,
I just wish you would have shown up more.
Are You There?
No answer...
Sitting in silence
Waiting,
But you never came.

Last Breath

I rose to the surface after being submerged
for almost 2 minutes.
Every time I'm under water I feel this sense
of relief.
The world around me ceases to exist,
And my body is finally at peace...
If only I could live below the surface,
When my lungs are left with no air is when I
feel the most alive, because I feel myself
fading, but I am fading into a blissful silence
where no one but I exists.

Loving You, Almost Killed Me

I was never the type of person who debated
on life or death;
Until I met you...
It was one thing after the other,
You destroyed my peace,
And dismantled the one place I could call
safe.
I still call you the angel of death,
Because loving you, almost killed me,
To the point where I thought I might have to
take my last breath.

You Made Me Believe Again

I never thought I would find myself here
again,
With these feelings I had left for dead.
Love became a stranger to me,
Your ice-cold skin did not allow me to see
that I could possibly fall in love again.

Waves

Being loved by you is a feeling I had never experienced.
Your love is so pure, something I never had before,
I know my heart made no mistake falling for a heart like yours.
As the waves crash, when we're close to the shore,
I wonder what our future will be like…

I want to dedicate this book to the
person who carried me for nine
months and who raised me to be the
person I am today; My mother, the
most beautiful flower in our family
garden.
I love you now, and forever.

To my brother, who fought so hard for
me to keep writing and never stopped
believing in me.

To my father
Who taught me to be strong and have
faith in gods timing.

Love always;
Angel Andrades Montanez

9 798868 911446